Yes You Can!
Fall in Love With Your New Home Purchase

© 2017 by DreamMaker Press
All Rights Reserved

DreamMaker Press, LLC
Denver, Colorado

ISBN- 978-1541035027

$14.99

First Printing

Team Work Makes the Dream Work

Don Loyd and Jo Hausman

If I were asked to name the chief benefit of the house, I should say:

The house shelters daydreaming,
The house protects the dreamer,
The house allows one
to dream in peace.

Gaston Bachelar

Disclaimer
The contents, discussions, legal and financial information and other materials contained in this book are for informational or educational purposes only and no content should be construed as, or relied upon as, legal, financial or investment advice; as the providing of legal, financial or investment services or as the recommendation of forms or of the opinions from author.

Introduction

At one time, and for many decades, homeownership was the proxy for the American dream. That all changed in 2008 with the crash of the housing market, and owning a home became a nightmare for many Americans. It became the "American Delusion," according to Grace W. Bucchianeri of the Wharton School of Business.

The good news is that the vagaries of the recession have passed, and Americans are once again getting into the housing market. Homebuyers are savvier this time around though, and go into the process better educated and armed with information. The recession taught some hard lessons, but lessons well learned.

This book contains some of the most information-packed information available. Our aim is to help you on your quest to learn everything you can about buying a home.

No matter how bad things were in the past, one thing hasn't changed: Buying a house is exciting! So let's get you going.

Chapter 1
Should I buy a Home?

It doesn't require tea leaves, a crystal ball or any other form of hocus-pocus to take the first step in determining if this is a good time to buy a home. While market conditions should play a role in your decision, the first step toward deciding whether to buy a home now or wait starts with you and the state of your finances.

The answer is, it depends. First, how's your credit? Lenders have tightened their FICO® requirements. Even FHA has raised the lower end of their acceptable FICO® range. How long have you been in your current job? Lenders now want to see at least two years with the same employer, and no decrease in income.

Next, do you have the cash to put down on a home? You'll need at least 20 percent of the list price of the home if you go with a lender. If you obtain an FHA-backed loan, the down payment requirement has a lot to do with your FICO® score.

That said, lending has become so tight that sometimes a stellar FICO® score can't make up for lower income, a spotty job record and even a huge down payment, according to recent news from the Wall Street Journal. If you're trying to time the market so that you purchase at the bottom, good luck. Nobody knows when it will bottom out. In fact, real estate agents in some parts of the country say their market has already hit bottom and is now on the way back up.

There are signs in the economy, according to some experts, that the real estate market may have a rosier near future than previously thought. These signs include:

> **Unemployment**

Housing market prognosticators keep a close eye on unemployment numbers. It's only natural that people worry more when their jobs aren't secure. This anxiety tends to make them hold off on spending money. Consumer confidence typically lags right along with low employment numbers. When the jobs situation improves, so does the confidence of Americans and money begins flowing again. So watch the unemployment numbers in your city because when they drop, housing prices may rise. But unemployment numbers only help us figure out part of the story.

> **Housing Inventory**

A "shrinking inventory" is a real estate term that describes a market in which the number of homes for sale decreases. Think of it as supply and demand. When there are fewer homes on the market, prices tend to rise, which is a good sign if you plan on selling your home.

But it's not a good sign for the homebuyer. First, prices go up when the inventory shrinks so you'll be forced to pay more if you wait. Then, there's the fact that there will be fewer homes on the market from which to choose. So, while a shrinking inventory may be a glimmer of hope for the health of the housing market, for you its proof that you waited too long to buy.

➤ New Housing Starts

Homebuilders sit out tight economies. When people are back to work and spending money again, builders begin new developments. While national new housing starts are important, keep an eye on your state's trends and those in your local area. While it's wise to monitor economic indicators to help time your home purchase to coincide with the bottom of the market, there's also a danger in that.

The only sure-fire way to know that we've hit the bottom of the market is when prices start rising. By then, it's too late. Real estate markets move in cycles and can take excruciatingly long to change, or transform almost overnight. The ideal time to buy a home is when both prices and interest rates are low.

Chapter 2
10 Best-Kept Secrets for Buying a Home

Get the most out of your money with these handy home-buying tips:

- **Keep Your Money Where It Is**

    It's not wise to make any huge purchases or move your money around three to six months before buying a new home. You don't want to take any big chances with your credit profile. Lenders need to see that you're reliable and they want a complete paper trail so that they can get you the best loan possible. If you open new credit cards, amass too much debt or buy a lot of big-ticket items, you're going to have a hard time getting a loan.

- **Get Pre-Approved for Your Home Loan**

There's a big difference between a buyer being pre-qualified and a buyer who has a pre-approved mortgage. Anybody can get pre-qualified for a loan. Getting pre-approved means a lender has looked at all of your financial information and they've let you know how much you can afford and how much they will lend you. Being pre-approved will save you a lot of time and energy so you are not running around looking at houses you can't afford. It also gives you the opportunity to shop around for the best deal and the best interest rates. Do your research: Learn about junk fees, processing fees or points and make sure there aren't any hidden costs in the loan.

> **Avoid a Border Dispute**

It's absolutely essential to get a survey done on your property so you know exactly what you're buying. Knowing precisely where your property lines are may save you from a potential dispute with your neighbors. Also, your property tax is likely based on how much property you have, so it is best to have an accurate map drawn up.

> **Don't Try to Time the Market**

Don't obsess with trying to time the market and figure out when is the best time to buy. Trying to anticipate the housing market is impossible. The best time to buy is when you find your perfect house and you can afford it. Real estate is cyclical, it goes up and it goes down and it goes back up again. So, if you try to wait for the perfect time, you're probably going to miss out.

> **Bigger Isn't Always Better**

Everyone's drawn to the biggest, most beautiful house on the block. But bigger is usually not better when it comes to houses. There's an old adage in real estate that says don't buy the biggest, best house on the block. The largest house only appeals to a very small audience and you never want to limit potential buyers when you go to re-sell. Your home is only going to go up in value as much as the other houses around you. If you pay $500,000 for a home and your neighbors pay $250,000 to $300,000, your appreciation is going to be limited. Sometimes it is best to is buy the worst house on the block, because the worst house per square foot always trades for more than the biggest house.

> **Avoid Sleeper Costs**

The difference between renting and home ownership is the sleeper costs. Most people just focus on their mortgage payment, but they also need to be aware of the other expenses such as property taxes, utilities and homeowner-association dues. New homeowners also need to be prepared to pay for repairs, maintenance and potential property-tax increases. Make sure you budget for sleeper costs so you'll be covered and won't risk losing your house.

> **You're Buying a House – Not Dating It**

Buying a house based on emotions is just going to break your heart. If you fall in love with something, you might end up making some pretty bad financial decisions.

There's a big difference between your emotions and your instincts. Going with your instincts means that you recognize that you're getting a great house for a good value. Going with your emotions is being obsessed with the paint color or the backyard. It's an investment, so stay calm and be wise.

➤ **Give Your House a Physical**

Would you buy a car without checking under the hood? Of course you wouldn't. Hire a home inspector. It'll cost a few hundred dollars, but could end up saving you thousands. A home inspector's sole responsibility is to provide you with information so that you can make a decision as to whether or not to buy. It's really the only way to get an unbiased third-party opinion. If the inspector does find any issues with the home, you can use it as a bargaining tool for lowering the price of the home. It's better to spend the money up front on an inspector than to find out later you have to spend a fortune.

➤ **The Secret Science of Bidding**

Your opening bid should be based on two things: what you can afford (because you don't want to outbid yourself), and what you really believe the property is worth. Make your opening bid something that's fair and reasonable and isn't going to totally offend the seller. A lot of people think they should go lower the first time they make a bid. It all depends on what the market is doing at the time.

You need to look at what other homes have gone for in that neighborhood and you want to get an average price per square foot. Sizing up a house on a price-per-square-foot basis is a great equalizer. Also, see if the neighbors have plans to put up a new addition or a basketball court or tennis court, something that might detract from the property's value down the road.

Today, so many sellers are behind in their property taxes and if you have that valuable information it gives you a great card to negotiate a good deal. To find out, go to the county clerk's office.

➢ Stalk the Neighborhood

Before you buy, get the lay of the land – drop by morning noon and night. Many homebuyers have become completely distraught because they thought they found the perfect home, only to find out the neighborhood wasn't for them. Drive by the house at all hours of the day to see what's happening in the neighborhood.

Do your regular commute from the house to make sure it is something you can deal with on a daily basis. Find out how far it is to the nearest grocery store and other services. Even if you don't have kids, research the schools because it affects the value of your home in a very big way. If you buy a house in a good school district versus bad school district even in the same town, the value can be affected as much as 20 percent.

The ache for home lives in all of us, the safe place where we can go as we are and not be questioned.

Maya Angelou

Chapter 3
A Guide to Buying Your First Home

Buying real estate, while once touted as a wise investment toward your future wealth, has become somewhat of a scary prospect to first-time buyers. The entire process is confusing; the market is a mess. Home buying is a process and, like any other, there are steps you should take to get you to your goal. While it's natural to be anxious about buying a first home, take the time to follow the steps and, before you know it, you'll be in your own home

➢ Financing Your New Home

One of the unpleasant tasks in the home buying process is figuring out how much house you can afford and then finding a lender to loan you money at an attractive rate and good terms. You'll need cash for the down payment and, unless you find a seller who is willing to help with them, the closing costs.

If you're on a tight budget, consider some of the government programs. The United States Department of Housing and Urban Development (HUD) backs low-cost, first-time homebuyer loans through the Federal Housing Administration (FHA). Aside from a conventional FHA-backed loan, you might want to consider purchasing a low-cost fixer-upper and using HUD's 203(k) program. This program provides one loan that pays for both the house and the work required to fix it.

No matter which route you decide to take, you'll need to shop for a loan. Take your time when looking for a loan, as rates and terms may vary widely between lenders.

> **Be a Smart Shopper Before Buying Your First Home**

Real estate buyer's agents will tell you that making a wish list is one of the most important steps to take before looking at houses. You'll actually make the list and then edit it several times. If you're half of a couple, you should both make your own lists.

Your original list should be an exercise in dreaming. Write down everything your ideal home would have – even if you think these items may be too expensive. Let your imagination run wild. After it's complete, go back over it with a more realistic eye. If you're on a tight budget, you may wish to cross off the stables and tennis courts.

Once you've whittled the list down so that it fits your real world, choose one or two items on which you will not compromise. Then, compare your list with your partner's. Anything that shows up on both lists is a "must have." That, along with your top must-have and your partner's can't-live-without, gives your agent a clear idea on which types of homes to show you and which to exclude.

Next, you'll need to decide on a neighborhood. If you have children, proximity to your chosen schools may be the deciding factor. Perhaps a location that provides for a quicker commute to work is your ideal. Decide on several areas and use RealEstate.com to run a quick check on housing prices to make sure you can afford to live there. Make a list of at least three neighborhoods that you're interested in seeing.

Now you're ready to choose an agent. That's where I come in. I have a list of referrals from clients who have used me in the past. So, give me a text me, or give me a call. When you meet with me, hand me your list of must-haves and the neighborhoods in which you wish to view houses, and let me get to work finding you a dream house.

> **You've Found a Home – Now What?**

Finding a house you wish to purchase is the first step toward what may be smooth sailing or an absolute nightmare. Prepare yourself for the worst and, if all goes well, consider yourself lucky.

First you'll make an offer. Determine what you want to offer on the house and then follow your agent's advice as to how appropriate the offer is. If the housing market is moving fast, with multiple offers on houses, make your highest and best offer at the outset, as you don't have time to bargain. If the market is slow, you may want to make a low offer and plan for some back-and-forth negotiating. Again, your agent is your best ally in this process.

Once the offer is accepted it's important to adhere to the time limits in the contract. Order your home inspection and shop for homeowner's insurance immediately. You hold the key to a smooth real estate transaction. By preparing adequately and choosing the right professionals to help you along the way, you guarantee your success. Welcome home!

> *Twenty years from now, you will be more disappointed by the things you didn't do than by the ones you did do.*
>
> Mark Twain

Chapter 4
5 Things to Consider When Buying a Home

The list of the features you want in your new home is personal and, no doubt, as long as your arm. The most important of these items are known as "hot buttons" in the real estate business, and not all buyers have the same ones.

From the must-have hardwood floors to the I'll-just-be-miserable-without-a-gourmet-kitchen, hot button lists help homebuyers narrow down the list of houses to view. If you're planning on buying a home, compile your list of what to look for, whittle it down to only those items on which you will not compromise, and then make sure your real estate agent gets a copy

1. **Put the Cart Before the Horse**

Figuring out how much house you can afford and then getting financing for your purchase are the first considerations when buying a home. Before you can look for that perfect kitchen, you need to make sure it fits in your budget. To determine what you can afford, you'll need to calculate your:

- current debt

- available cash for a down payment

- monthly income

- other ongoing monthly expenses

Some buyers check their credit reports and obtain their FICO® score to get an idea of where they stand financially. If there are only a few dings on your credit history, it's a good idea to take care of them before applying for a loan. Better credit means a lower rate on your mortgage loan.

I can take you to a Mortgage Broker who can sit down with you to review your credit. If it needs to improve before you apply for a loan, she can help you create a plan to help increase your credit score and chances of qualifying for a real estate loan. Trust me, it's not hard to do for most folk and it's pretty painless, too

2. Choosing Your Community

Choosing your ideal town or city is only part of the decision-making process. Now, it's time to narrow down the choice to a particular area, then a neighborhood or two. Local crime statistics can be had by visiting online sites such as the Department of Justice, or by placing a phone call to the local police department.

Drive through neighborhoods during different times of the day and week to look for traffic flow, noise levels and other activity. If you get lucky, you may find neighbors outdoors and you can stop and chat with them about what it's like to live in the neighborhood.

3. Don't Forget the Exterior Features

It's easy to be overwhelmed by a house you've fallen in love with and become blinded to the more practical aspects of actually owning it. Lot size and landscaping are important considerations when buying a home and often overlooked in favor of the home's interior. Who is going to mow that acre of lawn?

Are the trees going to lose their leaves every autumn, and, if so, do you think you'll be in the mood to dig out the rake and clean them up? Or, will gardener's fees be in your future? If so, you may need to do some research to determine the monthly cost of a gardener and add that to your potential house payment. The same goes for the pool. Pools require weekly to bi-weekly maintenance. If you don't know how to do it yourself, you'll need to hire someone, adding more to the monthly cost of owning the home.

4. Energy and Utilities Add Up

If you'll be moving to a new area you most likely aren't up to speed on how much residents typically pay for utilities every month. Depending on where you are buying a home, your power, gas and water bills may come as a shock.

Las Vegans, for instance, pay upwards of $300 a month to cool their homes in the summer – a $500 power bill is not out of the ordinary. Ask the seller how much she uses her utilities and what her average bills are. Power companies may also divulge this information.

If you are concerned about high energy costs, look for homes with improved weather-proofing, energy-efficient appliances and updated electrical wiring.

5. Consider Resale Value

This home may be the biggest investment you make in your life, so dig deep down inside to find your inner investor. Just as you wouldn't pour a ton of money into the stock market before performing due diligence, don't purchase a home purely on emotion.

Do some research to try to determine the home's future desirability. The city planning office is a good place to look for information. Ask about future development plans for the area. Nearby electric power plants, transformer stations and landfills may depreciate the value of the house you want to purchase, so consider carefully what may happen in the future.

Chapter 5
How Much Down Payment Do I Need for a House?

Lenders like to see the borrower have some skin in the game. With borrowers upside down on their homes simply mailing their keys back to the bank, and sticking lenders with negative equity rather than toughing out the down market and keeping their homes, lenders now want to know that you've got a personal stake in the deal.

By the way ... those "no money down" property flippers? The ones who were so obnoxious a few years ago? Yeah, those people and their amateur mortgage brokers are making your lattes at Starbucks now – and sending their tips to a bankruptcy trustee, in many cases.

As such, unless you fall into a couple of special categories, chances are you're going to have to come up with some cash as a down payment on your home.

Underwriting Standards Have Tightened

Don't count on trying to get cute. The days of trying to camouflage the fact that you have no personal stake in the property by taking out a piggyback loan to boost your down payment from 3 percent to 10 percent are pretty much over.

That didn't work out well for lenders, and we're in a back-to-basics market now. "Ever since the collapse, if you will, there's no real creative financing like there used to be four or five years ago," according to some of the real estate experts out there.

No Down Payments on VA Loans

You can still do a no-down payment mortgage via a Veterans Administration home loan. This is because the federal government stands behind the nation's veterans, guaranteeing the lender against loss if the veteran should default on the loan. VA home loans have the additional advantage of allowing the borrower to avoid paying primary mortgage insurance premiums, or PMI. This can easily save a borrower over $1,000 per year in many markets. Otherwise you'd have to pay these premiums until your loan-to-value ratio reached 80 percent.

The downside to VA loans is that, normally, you cannot discharge this debt in bankruptcy, as you can with other kinds of debt.

USDA

One alternative no-money-down option you may wish to explore: The USDA Rural Development Loan. This program will allow you to borrow up to 100 percent of the property, if you qualify, just like a VA loan. The program only covers homes in certain designated rural areas. Your family income must fall below 115 percent of the median income for your area.

Loans are for 30 years at a fixed rate of interest, and you can roll expected repair and improvement costs into the price of the loan. This isn't a giveaway program: You have to have decent credit to qualify.

Here's one down side to the USDA funds: Funding for this program tends to run out midway through the fiscal year, though. For best results, try to apply early in the U.S. government's fiscal year which begins October 1 every year.

How Much Down Payment is Needed for FHA Loans

If you obtain your loan under Federal Housing Administration (FHA) you may get into a home with just 3.5 percent down. This still means you'll need $7,000 in cash to put down on a $200,000 house, which can be a tough nut to crack for some borrowers.

However, FHA loans come with a handy twist: You can receive your down payment as a gift – say, from parents or a rich uncle – and still qualify for the loan. Your benefactor should be prepared to document the source of funds.

The Federal Housing Administration imposes limits on the loan amount, which vary according to the property's location. You can check the HUD website to find the FHA loan limit for your area.

The federal government has long allowed state governments and private charities to provide down payment assistance to those in need. In each case, you may be able to get some or all of your 3.5 percent down payment offset via one of these programs. Your mortgage representative or real estate agent may have more information on programs available in your area.

In both cases – VA loans and FHA loans – you will still have to come up with closing costs, which are frequently 3 or 4 percent of the loan on the buyer's side. The FHA, however, stipulates which closing costs the buyer can pay and the rest must be paid by the seller.

When you make your offer purchase a home, we can ask that the seller pay 3 or 4 percent of the purchase price for closing costs. If he accepts this provision in your offer, you have to come up with less cash to close. In a Buyer's market you can be pretty successful at receiving this concession.

Down Payments for Conventional Loans

A conventional loan, in nutshell, is any mortgage that doesn't come with a federal guarantee. We're back to the 5 percent to 20 percent down payment these days on conventional loans. Specifics vary with the lender and by location, as well as by whether the loan is "conforming," that is, within the underwriting standards established by Fannie Mae and Freddie Mac, the major mortgage buyers upstream from the lender.

To be honest, there are advantages to putting more money down: If you can reach the 20 percent threshold, you won't need to pay PMI. Plus, more home equity helps your credit score, counts as an asset on your balance sheet that you can actually borrow against (if you can qualify when you actually need the money!), and puts you in a better position to rent the property on a cash-flow positive basis if things don't break your way in the future.

What About Down Payments for Investment Properties

If the home is not your primary residence or a second home, then you can expect to have to come up with more – at least 20 percent, in most cases, depending on the nature of the property. Lenders require the higher down payment because mortgage insurance typically only covers primary residences. For the best interest rates, think closer to 25 percent or more – plus reserves against the possibility of vacancy.

If you want to hold your property in an IRA, then you may need to come up with at least 35 percent down, plus reserves, if you purchase and finance an investment house the traditional way. However, there may be nontraditional forms of purchasing investment homes in your IRA.

This subject is a specialized topic. If you need specialized information about financing an investment property, I can get you to a person who can answer your questions and help you build a strategy to accomplish that.

Chapter 6
The Importance of Loan Pre-Approval

Today loan pre-approvals are often more like the girlfriend or boyfriend from hell instead of a dream date come true – you can't live without them, but they can be a big headache too.

So how tough is it to pick up a loan pre-approval today, why are you just teasing yourself by attempting home shopping without one, and why is this the most important and controversial piece of paper since the pre-nup?

You Can't Get a Date Without a Pre-approval!

How critical is the importance of a loan pre-approval? You probably had a better chance of dating the hottest cheerleader or hunkiest quarterback at high school – back when you had pizza-like acne – than getting an appointment to even look at a home without a mortgage pre-qualification letter today.

Here's the reality: real estate agents will be reluctant to show homes to someone who has not qualified for a loan, it would be a waste of their time. You need to demonstrate that you have the funds available and/or appropriate credit for a purchase.

Save Yourself a Lot of Heartache

For homebuyers, the main importance of obtaining a loan pre-approval upfront ought to be recognizing that it can save a ton of time and crushed dreams. You don't want to take your partner out looking at their idea of a dream home only to have to downgrade them from a million dollar waterfront estate to a one-bedroom condo without a view.

Get pre-approved, find out how much you qualify for and then streamline your home search.

Note that just because you are approved for $X, that doesn't mean you have to or should max that number out. There are always unexpected extra bills, especially as a first-time homebuyer. It's better to sleep at night than to never be able to enjoy your new home and eventually lose it to foreclosure.

The Importance of a Pre-approval for Getting Offers Accepted

The best homes at the best prices always sell quickly and often receive several offers within hours of going on the market. Even if you have managed to get in to see a home without contacting a lender and getting pre-approved, no one is likely to take your offer until you have.

You don't want to miss out on your dream home because you kept putting it off. In reality most "pre-qualification" letters are completely worthless. You may not want to let your seller or agent in on this secret, but as a buyer you had better know it.

Most of you reading this have received a "pre-approved" offer of credit for something in the mail, only to find out you aren't when you respond. Unfortunately, the same principal applies here.

Loan officers and mortgage brokers desperate to capture your business and put new deals in their pipelines will often send you an official looking pre-approval letter based on a five minute phone conversation and a credit check. What this normally means is that, based on your statements about your income and assets and your credit score, you should qualify for a loan. In reality there are many more variables involved which won't be analyzed until you have made a formal application and some that may be specific to the property you are buying, which is unknown at the time of approval. In other words, they are worth less than the paper they are printed on.

The Importance of a Loan Pre-approval You Can Count On

While you may be fine with winging it, providing your offer gets accepted, an unreliable qualification letter can cost you big time. First, if your loan falls apart, you may lose thousands in deposit money. It could also mean paying a lot more than you expected in mortgage fees and rates after you are committed to buying. If you don't or can't buy or can't keep up with these higher payments, guess who ends up homeless?

How can you avoid this? No matter how busy you are, take the time to prepare and provide your lender with as much detailed information about your finances as possible, even if he doesn't ask for it. Provide W2s, tax returns, paystubs, bank statements, the works. This will help the lender identify and alert you to potential issues later.

You can't afford to be lazy – remember how much is on the line.

The house you looked at today and wanted to think about until tomorrow may be the same house someone looked at yesterday and will buy today.

Koki Adasi

Chapter 7
Defining Loan Types for Mortgages

If you're in the market for a house but don't have the savings to pay for the entire property with cash, you can get a residential mortgage to cover the difference between your down payment and the sale price of the house.

A residential mortgage is a common legal agreement in which an individual borrows money from a bank or person to buy property such as a house or a condominium. A mortgage agreement typically states that the borrower must repay the borrowed money and any interest to the lender on a predetermined schedule.

Should the borrower fail to pay per the contractual schedule, the lender typically has a legal right to take possession of or foreclose on the property. Below you'll find definitions of loan types for some of the most common mortgages available.

Fixed-Rate Mortgages

Fixed-rate mortgages are the safest bet if you always want to know what you owe. Generally repaid over a period of 15, 20 or 30 years, the interest rate and monthly payments of principal and interest for fixed-rate mortgages are locked in for the duration of the loan. If you can secure a fixed-rate mortgage, you limit the volatility of your loan and know exactly what your payment will be for the lifetime of the loan.

Adjustable-Rate Mortgage (ARM)

Also known as variable rate or tracker mortgages, adjustable rate mortgages are designed to adjust to match the market after an initial fixed rate period. For instance, a 5/1 arm will start to adjust to an index such as the one-year Treasury or the Cost of Funds Index after a five-year period at a fixed loan rate.

ARM loans can be appealing because they are often packaged with low initial rates, but once the rates adjust they can potentially cause dramatic and unpredictable swings in mortgage payments that are difficult to budget for.

Interest-Only Mortgage

If you expect your income to improve over time and are bullish on the real estate market and your ability to match a growing mortgage payment in the future or refinance, interest-only loans can be a good option. In the initial five- or ten-year period of the loan, the borrower only pays interest – no principal – meaning a smaller overall mortgage payment.

At the end of the interest-only period, either a balloon payment for the balance of the mortgage principal may be due or the payments may increase to pay off the principal within the remaining period of the loan. This type of loan is good for some.

This may not be your best option. Talk to your accountant before going this route.

Private Financing

Private financing, also referred to as private money, can be a good option for people who have been through bankruptcy, foreclosure or other financial troubles and are looking to buy a house. This is a financing method where a company or individual person may provide a mortgage loan to a non-conforming residential buyer who does not qualify for a bank loan.

These typically are considered high risk and therefore are likely to carry higher interest rates especially if the loans are high-risk. They are also largely unregulated. Lenders are required to comply with lending laws at the state and local level but not necessarily with banking regulations.

Seller Carryback and Hard Money Loan

Another option for properties that don't qualify for traditional bank financing but have a potential buyer with enough cash for a down payment, seller carryback and hard money loans are possible options for advancing a residential property sale. A seller carryback is when the seller of a property finances a percentage of a loan.

Hard money loan is when a mortgage is designed to cover just the loan-to-value ratio on a property. Typically, a down payment or some other kind of collateral is required from the borrower to secure this type of loan.

VA Loans

Only available to eligible service members who meet specific requirements, home loans from the Department of Veterans Affairs are popular among those who qualify as they require no down payment. Additionally, there are limits on lender feeds such as closing, origination and appraisal fees. No private mortgage insurance (PMI) is required to secure VA loans, even if service members opt not to provide a down payment.

FHA Loans

The Federal Housing Administration, a division of HUD, insures some types of loans to make homeownership more accessible through lower down payments and closing costs along with more flexible credit requirements. If you are buying a first home or a fixer-upper, you may be eligible for an FHA insured loan. The FHA also provides reverse mortgages for senior citizens who have paid off most of their mortgage and want to turn their home equity into cash for living expenses.

This is only the beginning! There are many other loan types for mortgages, including jumbo loans, second mortgages, reverse mortgages and rural development services loans. For more information on how to shop for loans and understand your rights as a homebuyer, talk to your independent Mortgage Broker.

Chapter 8
Applying For a Mortgage Loan

Buying a home is not something the average American does every day. While the purchase process is second nature to real estate and mortgage brokers, it is somewhat mysterious to the rest of us.

When asked how to eat an elephant, a wise person once responded, "one bite at a time." While the home loan process seems like a gargantuan task, it's easier to understand when it's broken down into smaller pieces.

Act Like a Boy Scout — Prepare

Wouldn't it be great if there were a one-stop shop where you could price-compare without having to run all over town? While a mortgage broker rather fits this bill, if you're more of a hands-on type of shopper, you'll need to do some legwork.

Before you go lender shopping, or, before you visit the lender you've chosen, get your paperwork in order so that you know exactly where you stand financially and how much house you can afford. Submitting all of the required paperwork in an organized fashion also helps speed along the approval process.

Although the lender will order your credit reports, if you're curious about where you stand, credit-wise, it's a good idea to order your own reports from all three credit reporting agencies. You are entitled to one free credit report annually and the Federal Trade Commission cautions consumers to order those reports from the only authorized source, AnnualCreditReport.com.

Obtain your FICO® score from the Fair Isaac Corporation (FICO®). This is the score lenders use and it's compiled from your credit reports. With the FICO® score and credit reports, you should be able to ascertain what type of mortgage loan you'll be offered.

Then, gather up the necessary paperwork for the lender. Ask the lender exactly what you need to bring with you to the application appointment. Although this list is far from exhaustive, when you apply for mortgage loan the typical lender requires:

- Copies of your last two tax returns
- Bank and investment account statements from the last two months
- A copy of your current mortgage papers or your landlord's contact information if you are a renter
- Written explanations for any late payments or other negative marks on your credit report
- A copy of your Social Security card and driver's license
- Account numbers, balances and payments on any loans, credit cards, car loans, personal loans, student loans or other obligations

- ➤ Verification of your income, such as pay stubs
- ➤ Divorce information if you're making or receiving alimony or child support payments
- ➤ Veteran certificate of eligibility and DD214, if applicable
- ➤ Copies of bankruptcy papers, if applicable
- ➤ A copy of your purchase agreement if you've made an offer on a new home

Steps to Mortgage Loan Approval

Depending on the housing market in your area and the lender's policies, getting a mortgage loan can be surprisingly quick, or it can be a somewhat lengthy process. Some mortgage loans may even get same-day approval if your credit is good and you meet requirements for the down payment and income-to-debt ratio.

Applying for a mortgage loan typically involves the following steps:

1. **Application:** You submit a home loan application form, along with documentation

2. **Verification:** The lender turns your loan package over to its processing department where all of the information included in the application is verified. From there, it goes to the underwriter who makes the decision whether or not to approve the loan.

3. **Good Faith Estimate:** The lender has three days after your application is submitted to supply you with a Good Faith Estimate (GFE), outlining the costs of the

mortgage loan. You will also receive a Truth In Lending Disclosure, outlining the expected monthly payment, the APR and a list of all finance charges.

4. **Approval:** Once the loan is approved, the lender will send a commitment letter. This letter basically reiterates the information contained in the GFE and the Truth in Lending Disclosure. It also contains a deadline, or commitment period, after which the terms may change. The borrower typically needs to return a signed copy of this to the lender before the end of the commitment period. Read the letter carefully before doing so. If you have any questions about anything in the letter, run it by your attorney.

The time period from application to approval can stressful for the buyer. There may be requests for more information or other delays. In some areas, the shortage of appraisers can be a delaying issue. Being fully prepared when you apply for a mortgage loan goes a long way in alleviating future problems and toward relieving your stress.

Preparation and patience - good words to live when applying for a home loan.

Chapter 9
How to Pick a Champion Mortgage Broker

Today you don't need just another loan officer. Your quest to choose the right mortgage broker is about finding a bold champion who will go to battle for you.

Contrary to the popular misconception that getting approved for a home loan is simply a matter of credit scores and figures, today it is often more like entering a gladiator's arena.

Besides battling against increasingly tougher lending and credit guidelines, knowing how to pick a great mortgage broker will protect you from bait and switch tactics, unscrupulous lenders who will demand a larger down payment at the last minute and will ensure you close on time, protecting your deposit money. We aren't just talking about the difference in being approved or denied, or a few extra dollars a month, but your ability to buy or retain your home and tens or even hundreds of thousands of dollars.

Those who want to know how to really pick a mortgage broker who will blaze the way to a great home loan victory need to be on the lookout for the following qualities.

- ➢ Reputable and honorable

- ➢ Skilled and experienced

- ➢ Brave and courageous

How to Pick an Honorable Mortgage Broker

Signs of a Shady Lender: When to Run Away

    A. You are quoted an interest rate without being asked detailed questions.

    B. You are rushed into applying or having your credit pulled.

    C. You are asked for any type of money upfront.

    D. The broker tells you everything you want to hear.

Signs of Reputable Mortgage Brokers

    A. They are members of professional associations like the Chamber of Commerce and local chapter of the National Association of Mortgage Brokers.
    B. What are others saying about them? Check the Better Business Bureau, consumer comment sites like Yelp, and Google them. Remember that people will always complain; it is how these complaints are handled that really counts.
    C. Check their mortgage broker license status with the state online.
    D. They will sit down and try to understand your individual goals and situation to match you with the best possible loan for your personal needs as well as presenting a variety of options.

How to Pick a Skilled Mortgage Broker

Just having a mortgage broker's license or working for a big name bank doesn't automatically make someone a skilled mortgage broker. It can take years to learn the ins and outs of the business and how to get the best deals for consumers. No book knowledge accurately prepares a mortgage broker for what it takes to get loans closed. You want a battle-tested champ who has honed his or her skills on the front lines.

Getting your loan approved means mastery of volumes of information as well as talented technical skills at bringing together appraisals, title searches, insurance and loan programs, and all of the many, many people involved at every level. The truth is that getting your loan approved is often about who your mortgage broker knows.

It can take a while to build these relationships, but once they have been in the business for a few years they can get head underwriters on the phone and V.P.s who can override senseless underwriting conditions to get your loan request expedited.

Find out how long the broker has been in the business, and test him or her out with a few questions. Does she respond quickly? Can he give you answers on the spot? Is she proactive about helping you to avoid potential issues?

How to Pick a Champion Mortgage Broker

What really makes the difference between a champion mortgage broker and the rest is that he is motivated and willing to go to battle for you. She won't lay down and accept a denial and she won't accept delays from your appraiser, title company or insurance agent.

He will fight to get you the best loan possible and ensure

Yes You Can! Fall in Love With Your New Home Purchase

your closing happens on time. You want the Conan the Barbarian of mortgage brokers on your side.

How to identify them?

1. They won't be afraid to turn away your business if you insist on just getting quoted a rate instead of allowing them to find out what you really qualify for.

2. They won't just tell you what you want to hear to get your business.

3. They can be overheard hammering an underwriter on the phone and educating them about how the guidelines should be interpreted.

4. There are great home loans out there to be had, and interest rates have certainly never been better. So choose your champion mortgage broker, and have him or her help you purchase the home of your dreams or slash your housing payments.

Chapter 10
What Does Buying a House on Contingency Mean?

When it comes to real estate contracts for buying or selling a home, contingencies hold the key to either big savings or large potential loses. What do you need to know about them?

Gambling on Contingencies

A contingency is a condition (or clause). In other words, you are making an offer to buy a home provided certain conditions are met. The more contingencies the better for buyers; they provide more opportunities to walk away, ensuring a refund of the deposit money if something turns up they don't like. However, demand too many contingencies and your offer could get shot down by sellers who are afraid you may walk away

As a homebuyer the main questions is how many contingencies can you get away with in your offer to purchase a home? What's more important to you? Making sure you land this home and make your partner happy or making sure you don't end up losing your precious capital? What you can get away with often depends on current market conditions.

What Contingencies Should I Include in My Purchase Offer?

There are many potential contingencies that you may want to include in your offer. In fact, buyers can dream up almost any contingency they feel like. Whether it gets accepted can be a completely different story, though.

The most common, and the answer you will most often receive when asking, "What does buying a house on contingency mean?" is an offer contingent on the buyer selling his or her current home. Few people want to take on a new mortgage until they have rid themselves of their old one.

This makes sense, but in the past it has led to long chains of contingent contracts, which could easily crumble if one link is broken. This means it is highly unlikely you will get an offer like this accepted unless you can prove your home is already under contract and the buyer's financing is approved.

Five more common contingencies to contemplate:

1. Appraisal Contingency

Appraisal contingencies state that the buyer is entitled to cancel a contract and receive a refund of their deposit if the property does not appraise for a minimum amount (normally the purchase price).

2. Financing Contingency

This is perhaps one of the most useful for buyers and the easiest to manipulate. This makes the contract contingent on the buyer's ability to obtain financing at a certain loan-to-value, interest rate and term. If not, the buyer may cancel, and if the buyer can't provide proof of a mortgage commitment in a specified period of time, the seller can boot them too. However, making an offer contingent on 100 percent financing at a 4 percent rate is unlikely to get accepted. While an offer specifying a 70 percent LTV and a max rate of 7 percent is going to be much more attractive.

3. Inspections

This gives the buyer an out should the required repairs be found to exceed a specific dollar amount or percentage of the purchase price. However, most bank-owned properties are now sold almost exclusively on an "as-is" basis

4. Zoning

Investors looking for bargains on properties that can hold big profits if the usage can be altered will want to use a zoning contingency. Getting your hands on a prime lot, which now holds a single family home but which could allow for a condo building or hotel, could produce massive potential.

5. Spousal or Partner Approval

Speed is essential today. Offers can stack up in hours and if yours isn't in, you could either be stuck in a bidding war or just flat out of luck. Making your offer contingent on your spouse's or partner's viewing of the property can make sure you are in the running without committing 100 percent. This allows investors to confirm hunches on the potential value and has probably saved many marriages as well.

The Secret Golden Clause

A "kick out" clause is used when a contract is contingent on selling the buyer's current home. It allows the seller to continue to market the home to other buyers. If a qualified buyer makes an offer on the home, the seller gives the previous buyer a time limit to either remove or exercise the contingency.

The kick-out clause must be carefully drafted to protect the seller. This is one of those situations where a real estate attorney should be consulted.

Making Backup Offers

What does buying a house on contingency mean for others who are interested? You shouldn't just pass over homes you like because they are already under contract. Deals fall apart all the time for all types of reasons, especially when they have many contingencies. If you like it, ask your real estate agent to submit a backup offer or perhaps you can even get the current offer kicked out!

> *A Realtor® is not a salesperson. They're a matchmaker. They introduce people to homes until they fall in love with one. Then they're a wedding planner.*
>
> Lydia

Chapter 11
How to Choose a Buyer's Agent

Although Americans are smitten with the DIY craze, buying real estate is not a do-it-yourself project. Sure, it's fine to surf the Internet to search for your dream home, but when it comes time to actually view the homes, make sure you are fully represented by your own real estate agent.

Many new homebuyers don't understand that although it may be perfectly legal in your state for the seller's agent to also represent the buyer, it isn't wise. This situation is known as "dual agency," a type of transaction that at one time was outlawed in all 50 states, and here's why: The seller's real estate agent has a duty to his or her client to act in the client's best interests.

Now, how can this happen in a dual agency situation when the seller's interests and the buyer's interests are the exact opposite? Although agents feel they can offer the same ethical treatment to both parties, it doesn't always happen. To protect your interests during the purchase process, secure your own representation. It costs you, as the buyer, nothing. The seller pays the buyer's agent's commission out of the proceeds of the sale.

Do I need a "Buyer's" Agent?

If having an agent who deals only with buyers is important to you, you will want a great Buyer's Agent who work solely for buyers, avoiding the conflicts of interest inherent in the traditional seller-oriented purchase transactions.

There are several situations in which you absolutely must choose an agent who is a bona fide specialist:

- The purchase of a luxury home
- The mobile home purchase
- Buying a short sale
- The purchase of ranch property
- Actually, you should always use a Buyer's Broker when purchasing real property

Aside from these situations, pursue the best agent for your needs.

Get Referrals

Whether you need a real estate agent to list your home for sale or to assist you with buying a home, a referral is the best way to find one. Ask everyone you know, including family members, co-workers, neighbors, friends and local business people.

The checkout lady at the grocery store may have just purchased a home and adores her agent. So don't neglect to ask everyone you come into contact with and start compiling a list of names.

What if you're relocating to an area and don't have a network of contacts there? There are several other ways to find the perfect real estate agent for your needs:

> Online: The larger real estate sites, such as RealEstate.com, offer the opportunity to search for real estate agents in your area. At RealEstate.com, scroll to the bottom of the home page and click on "Professionals."

> Relocation Representative: If you work for a large company and find yourself relocating as a result of this employment, consult the employee relocation representative for a list of agents to interview.

> Chamber of Commerce: Call the Chamber of Commerce located in the area where you are moving. The folks there typically have a directory of members and will be happy to refer you to several agents in the area.

Ask the Right Questions

Most guides to choosing the right real estate agent will counsel you to find out if the agent is full-time or part-time and suggest that you go with the full-time agent. The thinking behind this suggestion is that the full-time agent will have more time for you.

Not so fast. Ask a follow-up question: How big is your staff? The superstar agent with a staff of 15 is the agent you will probably never speak with or see until closing, if then. That's not to say this person isn't a good agent, but to remind you that if you're looking for personal, one-on-one interaction with the agent you hire, don't hire the superstar with a huge staff. If, on the other hand, you're looking for speed and efficiency, the agent with a large staff is typically better able to provide that.

Ask the agent how many other clients he or she is currently working with. The more clients the agent has, the thinner his or her attention is spread. If you find a house online that you absolutely love, time is of the essence in a fast-moving market. Will the agent have time to accommodate your last-minute showing needs?

If it's important to you that the agent has a certain amount of experience, by all means ask how long he has been in the business. Keep in mind, however, that new agents typically work securely under the wing of their brokers, so you are actually getting the wisdom and benefit of a highly experienced real estate pro, although second-hand.

As important as it is to ask the right questions, listening to the agent is equally as important. What types of questions does the agent ask? One of the most important is whether or not you have loan pre-approval. The savvy real estate agent understands that until you have seen a lender, looking at available homes is a waste of time, both yours and hers. Reject any agent who doesn't pose this question.

Should I Sign an Agreement?

Many agents who consider themselves buyer specialists will ask that you sign a broker's agreement. This document commits you to working exclusively with the agent for a pre-determined amount of time. Broker's agreements typically state that the agent will be compensated in the event the buyer switches to another agent and ends up purchasing a home shown by the original agent.

If the agent insists that you sign an agreement, ask for a short-term commitment. This way, should you decide the relationship between the two of you isn't working out; you're only locked into working with her for a short time. Agents typically ask for a 90-day commitment but the terms are negotiable, so choose a time period that you are comfortable with.

You are also within your rights to ask for a guarantee. Request that a clause be inserted into the agreement stating that if either party decides the business relationship isn't a good fit, they will be released from the agreement.

Getting your finances in order and securing funding for the purchase of your home should always be the first steps in your home buying process. Finding the right real estate agent, while second on the to-do list is no less important.

What to Expect from Your Buyer's Agent

If you're going into the home purchase process well armed with information, you already know how important it is to use your own real estate agent and not the seller's.

Real estate agents owe their clients what is known as a "fiduciary duty." Although it sounds like legal jargon, it simply means that the agent is obligated to act in the best interests of his or her client.

What are these interests? At their most basic, the seller's interest is to sell the home for the most money possible while the buyer is interested in purchasing the home for the least amount of money possible. Of course, both parties have ancillary interests such as the protection of their privacy.

The fact is, a seller's interests and a buyer's interests are completely different and, in fact, conflict with one another. Let's take a look at some of the specific interests that a real estate agent's fiduciary duty includes.

Full Disclosure

Above and beyond the homeowner's disclosures, the real estate agent must disclose all information he or she has that is relevant to the principal's interests. This includes any facts the agent may have about the value or desirability of the home and any knowledge about the other party that may affect negotiations.

An example of the duty to disclose is the seller's agent that finds out, somehow, that the buyer is willing to pay more than what he originally offers. Since the agent has a fiduciary duty to the seller, she must disclose this fact.

Suppose the buyer's agent knows that the seller is going through a divorce and is highly motivated to sell the home quickly. This is valuable information for his client and must be disclosed.

Confidentiality

Hand in hand with disclosing the opposing party's secrets comes a duty to protect those of the principal. If the seller's client is motivated to sell the home because of a job transfer, yet wants this information kept from the buyer, his agent has a duty to keep the information confidential.

Absolute Obedience

Real estate agents are obligated to obey all client instructions, as long as these instructions are legal. The seller's agent is obligated to follow the instructions of only the seller and the buyer's agent is obligated only to the buyer.

Loyalty

The duty of loyalty demands that the real estate agent act solely in the best interests of the principal to the exclusion of all other interests, including his or her own. In layperson's terms, loyalty means that the seller's agent must do everything he or she can to gain an advantage for the seller. The same applies to the buyer's agent and the buyer.

While the above doesn't include all fiduciary duties of a real estate agent, it includes those most important to the consumer. As you can see, the seller and the buyer have competing interests, creating competing duties for their agents. This is why, even though in many states it is legal for an agent to represent both parties in the transaction (known as dual agency), it is not wise for the agent or the consumer.

There is no shortage of real estate agents in this country. Furthermore, the seller pays the buyer's agent's fees, so there is no reason not to have your own real estate agent.

What Else Should You Expect From Your Real Estate Brolker/Agent?

- ➢ Search for appropriate homes – If you've told your agent you want three bedrooms and two bathrooms and she keeps showing you homes with 1 bathroom, your agent isn't paying attention to your needs.

- ➢ Help determine value – Your agent should compile a comparative market analysis for any home on which you would like to make an offer. This helps you determine if the list price is appropriate and how much money to offer for the home.

- ➢ Disclosure – Aside from the agent's fiduciary duty to disclose what he knows about the other party, he also has a duty to disclose any property defects that he has observed.

- ➢ Purchase agreement – Your agent should explain to you the entire purchase agreement before asking you to sign it. The agreement should be constructed in a manner that protects your interests and meets your needs.

- ➢ Counter offer – Should the seller counter your offer or you need to amend the purchase agreement to request repairs, your agent should fully explain the process and advise you to seek legal counsel, if appropriate, to ensure your protection.

➢ Acceptance – Once your offer is accepted your agent should offer advice about obtaining a home inspection and other inspections that may be specific to the region, remain in contact with the title company and the lender to ensure that all time limits are met, and attend the closing with you.

Real estate agents who are members of the National Association of Realtors® (NAR) are the only agents allowed to call themselves Realtors®. NAR has its own set of ethics that Realtors® swear to uphold in addition to their statutory fiduciary duties.

Glossary

A

Abstract
> A succinct summary; (for example, an abstract of judgment; an abstract of title, an abstract plant.)

Abstract of Judgment
> Summary of a court judgment creating a lien against a property when filed with the county recorder.

Abstract of Title
> The condensed history of a title to a particular parcel of real estate, consisting of a summary of the original grant and all subsequent conveyances and encumbrances affecting the property and a certification by the abstractor that the history is complete and accurate.

Abstract Plant
> A collection of information and documents relating to title of a particular property. Also known as "titleplant."

Acceleration Clause
> The clause in a mortgage or deed of trust that can be enforced to make the entire debt due immediately if the borrower defaults on an installment payment or other covenant.

Acceptance
> The written approval made by the seller from a buyer's offer.

Accrued
> On a closing statement, items of expense that are incurred but not yet payable, such as interest on a mortgage loan or taxes on real property.

Addendum
> Any addition or change to a contract.

Adjustable Rate Mortgage (ARM)
> A loan with an interest rate that fluctuates based on a specified financial index, such as Treasury securities or the 11th District Cost of Funds.

Agent
> A licensed representative of the state to conduct real estate transactions.

Agreement of Sale
> Also known as an agreement to convey. A signed, written contract entered into between the seller (vendor) and buyer (vendee) for sale of real property (land) under certain specific terms and conditions.

Alienation
> The transfer of property from one person to another. Alienation may be voluntary, such as by gift or sale, or involuntary, as through eminent domain or adverse possession.

Alienation Clause
A term of a mortgage requiring that the borrower
> pay in full the principal and interest due upon the sale of the property. (*See Acceleration or Due-on-Sale Clause*)

All-Inclusive Deed of Trust
> A form of deed of trust that, in addition to any other amounts actually financed, includes the amounts of any prior deeds of trust. Sometimes referred to as a wrap-around or over-riding trust deed.

Amortization
> Amortization is a schedule that outlines your loan payments for the duration of a loan. It details how much of each monthly payment goes toward the principal and how much goes toward paying off the loan balance. Initially, the bulk of your payments will be applied toward the interest. Many banks and title companies offer free amortization books. Be sure to ask for your copy. They're a handy tool.

Appraisal
> Generally paid for by the buyer, the appraisal provides an estimate of a property's worth. Required by most lenders, it must be performed by a licensed appraiser before your home loan will be approved. The appraiser will arrive at a value based on the sale price of similar property. That is called "comparable" value.

Appraise
> To fix or set a price or value upon.

Appreciation
> The difference between the increased value of the property and the original value.

Arrears
> Generally, being overdue in an installment payment.

Assessor

> A municipality employee who estimates the value of properties for the purpose of taxes.

Assignee
> The person to whom a transfer of interest is made. Hence, an assignee of an Agreement of Purchase and Sale may buy the property and enforce the contract in the same fashion as the original party.

Assignment
> The method by which a right or contract is transferred from one person (the assignor) to another (the assignee).

Assignor
> The person who makes an assignment to another person.

Assumable Mortgage
> A mortgage that can be taken over ("assumed") by the buyer when a home is sold. If interest rates have risen, an assumable mortgage at a low rate may prove a selling point for the property.

B
Balloon Payment
> A final payment of a mortgage loan that is considerably larger than the required periodic payments because the loan amount was not fully amortized.

Bankruptcy
An action filed in a federal bankruptcy court that
> allows a creditor to reorganize or discharge credit obligations due to insolvency. A property owner may halt foreclosure action by filing bankruptcy. Bankruptcies remain on a credit record for 7 years

and can severely limit a person's ability to borrow.

- Chapter 7—"Debtor Wipeout." The court oversees the liquidation of the debtors' nonexempt assets, distributing the cash proceeds proportionally among creditors.

- Chapter 11—A Chapter 11 is a business reorganization proceeding.

- Chapter 13—"Debtor Workout." A Workout is the almost-automatic choice of most trustors seeking to use a bankruptcy filing to delay the inevitable trustee's sale as long as they can. The purpose of this proceeding is to give a wage earner time for rehabilitation . . . a temporary respite free from the collection efforts of creditors.

Beneficiary
:   A person entitled to receive money or assets from a trust or an estate. A lender is a beneficiary with a deed of trust or a note as a security for a loan.

Betterment
:   Any improvement of real estate that results in a rise in market value of that property.

Bid
:   An offer by an intending purchaser to pay a designated price for property that is about to be sold at auction.

Bill of Sale
:   Written document by which title to personal property (goods or chattels) is transferred from one party to another.

Blanket Deed of Trust
> A deed of trust secured by more than one lot or parcel of land.

Borrower
> The individual to whom a thing or money is lent at his request.

BPO
> Brokers Price Opinion.

Breach
> The breaking or violating of a law, a right, obligation, engagement, or duty, either by commission or omission.

Broker
> An agent authorized by the state to deal in real estate.

Brokerage
> The bringing together of two or more parties interested in making a real estate transaction.

Buy-Down mortgage
> A financing technique used to reduce the monthly payments for the first few years of a loan. Funds in the form of discount points are given to the lender by the builder or seller to buy down or lower the effective interest rate paid by the buyer, thus reducing the monthly payments for a set time.

Buyer's Broker (*Buyer's Agent, Buyer's Representative*)
> A Buyer Broker, as opposed to a Listing Broker, represents only the interests of the buyer. For a broker (also referred to as agent sometimes) to be considered

a buyer's broker, an agreement must be made between the buyer and the broker. Without such an agreement, the agent could end up representing the seller in a real estate transaction. In most states we now have what's call "Limited Dual Agency." Under this theory, a broker can represent both the buyer and the seller.

Buyers Market
> A market condition where there are fewer buyers than there are sellers. Usually indicated when a property is on the market for more than 90 days and interest rates are very high. (12 percent or higher)

C

Capital Gain
> A profit earned from the sale of an asset.

Cash Flow
> The surplus after paying operating expenses and mortgage payments.

Certificate of Sale
> A certificate issued at a judicial sale entitling the buyer to receive a deed after confirmation of court for the purchase of the property.

Chain of Title
> A succession of conveyances comprising the title record history to a specific parcel of real property. Chattel Personal property, such as household items.

Chattel Mortgage
> A mortgage secured by personal property.

Closing Costs

This is the final step in the home buying/selling process. The loan documents are signed and finalized at this point. After the documents are signed, notarized, and the money submitted to satisfy all the debts, the transfer of the deed is made from the buyer to the seller when the title company (or attorney) files the deed and any supporting documentation with the country clerk. The filing of the documents with the county clerk signifies closing has occurred.

Closing Date
> The agreed-upon date for a buyer to take over property.

Cloud on Title
> Any outstanding claim that contradicts the title record, and if valid, would impair the owner's title.

Code
> A collection of laws relating to a certain topic, such as real property or patents.

Cosigner
> A cosigner signs a promissory note and takes responsibility for the debt.

Collateral
> Real estate or personal property pledged as security for a debt.

Collection
> Obtaining payment or the liquidation of a debt or claim, either by personal solicitation or legal proceedings.

Comparables

Similar properties used as yardsticks to determine the market value of a certain property.

Complaint
The original or initial pleading by which an action is commenced; a written statement of the essential facts constituting the offense charged.

Condemnation
A judicial or administrative proceeding to exercise the power of eminent domain, through which a government agency takes private property for public use and compensates the owner.

Contingency
A specified condition that must be fulfilled before a contract becomes firm and binding.

Contract
An agreement between two or more persons creating an obligation to do or not to do a particular thing.

Conventional Loan
A loan that requires no insurance or guarantees.

Conveyance
A written instrument that transfers title to or an interest in land from one party to another (for example, a deed, an assignment, or a bill of sale)

Counteroffer
A response given to an offer.

Credit report
A document from a credit bureau setting forth a credit rating and pertinent financial data concerning a person or a company and used by banks,

merchants, suppliers and the like in evaluating a credit risk.

Creditor
One to whom money is owed.

D
Debt
A sum of money due by a certain and express agreement; a specified sum of money owing to one person from another, including not only obligation of debtor to pay but the right of the creditor to receive and enforce payment.

Debt Ratio
To compare the total monthly payments of all of the borrower's debts (including the mortgage) with the gross monthly income of the borrower. It evaluates the borrower's ability to pay mortgage. Also referred to as Debt-to-Income ratio.

Debtor
An entity that owes a debt; one who owes a debt.

Decree of Foreclosure
A court order to set out the outstanding amount on a delinquent mortgage in order to sell the property to pay the mortgagee.

Deed
A written instrument that, when executed and delivered, conveys title to or an interest in real estate.

Deed in Lieu of Foreclosure
A process whereby the owner, with the approval of the lender, deeds the property to the lender to avoid foreclosure. Lenders are generally reluctant to

accept a deed in lieu unless the title is free and clear of any other encumbrances junior to theirs and the owners execute an estoppel affidavit acknowledging that they are acting volitionally, with informed consent.

Deed of Reconveyance
> An instrument that releases and discharges a deed of trust, when the mortgage has been paid out.

Deed of Trust (Trust Deed)
> A three party security instrument conveying the legal title to real property as security for the repayment of a loan. The owner is called the trustor. The neutral third party to whom the bare legal title is conveyed (and who is called on to liquidate the property if need be) is the trustee. The lender is the beneficiary. When the loan is paid off, the trustee is directed by the beneficiary to issue a deed of reconveyance to the trustor, which extinguishes the trust deed lien.

Default
> The failure to make payments in full on time or at all or to live up to any other obligations placed on the borrower by the loan agreement.

Defeasance Clause
> A clause used in leases and mortgages that cancels a specified right upon the occurrence of a certain condition, such as cancellation of a mortgage upon repayment of the mortgage loan.

Defendant
> The person who defends against a claim asserted in a court action.

Deficiency Judgment
> A judgment entered in a lawsuit when a property is sold for less than the amount of the loan.

Delinquency
> A condition when the payment is late but not yet in default.

Demand Letter
> Also known as a Breach Letter or Notice of Intent to Foreclose. Notice to the borrower that he/she is in "breach" of the terms of the Note and advising of the right to cure the default.

Department of Housing and Urban Development (HUD)
> A federal agency focusing on programs regarding housing and renewal of city communities.

Department of Veterans Affairs (VA)
> An independent federal agency overseeing programs for military veterans, including loan and mortgage programs. This agency allows most veterans to purchase a house without a down payment.

Disclosure Statement
> Document disclosing the terms of a loan.

Due-on-Sale Clause
> A clause in a mortgage that requires that the mortgage be paid out in full upon the sale of the property.

Due Diligence
> Such a measure of prudence, activity, or assiduity as is properly to be expected from a reasonable and prudent man under the particular circumstance.

E
Earnest Money Deposit
> Along with an offer, buyers can make a deposit on the home to demonstrate the seriousness of the offer. When an earnest money deposit is made, it is held by an escrow until closing. It is then added to the down payment.

Easement
> A right of way allowing someone to cross over another's property for certain purposes, such as power lines or water mains.

Encroachment
> A fixture that illegally intrudes into or invades the property or encloses a portion of it, diminishing its width or area.

Encumbrance
> Anything, such as a mortgage, tax, or judgment lien, an easement, or restriction on the use of the land or an outstanding dower right that may diminish the value or use and enjoyment of a property.

Equity
> The surplus of value that may remain after existing liens are deducted from the property.

Equity Right of Redemption
> The right to avoid foreclosure action by paying off the debts, interest, and fees that accumulated on the property.

Escrow Account
> Funds held before closing by a third party, usually including the earnest money deposit. Future taxes

and homeowners insurance, held by the mortgage company after closing, are also considered escrow.

Estate
> The total assets a person has when he dies, including real property.

Estoppel Certificate
> A certificate in which a borrower certifies the amount owed on a mortgage loan and the rate of interest.

Eviction
> The act of depriving a person of the possession of land or rental property held or leased.

F

Fair Market Value
> The amount at which property would change hands between a willing buyer and a willing seller, neither being under any compulsion to buy or sell and both having reasonable knowledge of the relevant facts.

Fannie Mae
> It's an official name of the Federal National Mortgage Association, which is one of the largest agencies that buys mortgages from lenders and resells them as securities on the secondary mortgage market.

FHA – Federal Housing Administration
> FHA is a branch of the Department of Housing and Urban Development (HUD). The agency's basic function is to direct housing in a way that Congress mandates by issuing mortgage insurance to institutional lenders on the loans they make. With such loan insurance, lenders are willing to lend with smaller down payments and at lower rates of interest.

FHA Loans
> A loan program offering low-rate mortgages to buyers willing to make a down payment as little as 3 percent.

First Mortgage
> A mortgage that is in first position and has priority as a lien over all other mortgages.

FSBO – For Sale By Owner
> This term refers to property being sold without a real estate broker. FSBO is also used to refer to the homeowner who is selling the property.

Foreclosure
> A legal procedure whereby property used as security for a debt is sold to satisfy the debt in the event of default in payment of the mortgage note or default of other terms in the mortgage document. The foreclosure procedure brings the rights of all parties to a conclusion and passes the title in the mortgaged property to either the holder of the mortgage or a third party who may purchase the realty at the foreclosure sale, free of all encumbrances affecting the property subsequent to the mortgage.

G

Garnishment
> A statutory proceeding whereby a person's property, money, credits in possession or under the control of, or owing by, another are applied to payment of the former's debt to third person by proper statutory process against debtor and garnishee.

Good Faith Estimate
Institutional lender estimates the costs a borrower

will incur, including inspection fees and loanprocessing charges.

Grace Period
> A period of days during which a debtor may cure a delinquency without penalty (before triggering a late charge, a foreclosure, or an acceleration of the balance due).

Grantee
> The person to whom the title of the property is granted.

Grantor
> The person (seller) who grants title to another person (buyer).

H

Habendum Clause
> Meaning "to have and to hold," which defines the quantity of the estate transferred to the new owner of land.

Home Equity Line of Credit
> Sometimes referred to as an HELOC, a Home Equity Line of Credit is a loan that a property owner secures that can be repaid and borrowed again at the owner's convenience.

Home Equity Loan
> Borrowing against the equity in one's home.

HUD 1 Statement
> A form, usually given by a bank, that includes the costs of purchasing a home.

Hypothecate
> When you use something as security and still retain possession of it.

I
Indemnify
> Any losses and damages an individual endures for which you are fully responsible.

Instrument
> A legal written document.

Involuntary lien
> A lien issued against a property without an owner's approval.

J
Joint Ownership
> When two or more parties own the same property.

Joint Venture
> A project where two or more individuals take part in a business transaction to share the cost, risk, and reward.

Judgment
> The final decision of the court resolving a dispute and determining the rights and obligations of the parties.

Notes

Notes

Notes

Notes

Notes

Notes

Notes

Notes

Notes

Notes

www.ingramcontent.com/pod-product-compliance
Lightning Source LLC
Chambersburg PA
CBHW061157180526
45170CB00002B/840